Kick Ass Red Lipstick

by Cat Cantrill

Jenna—

I cannot thank you enough for allowing me to run for WOTF—

I am so blessed to know you and be on this journey with you. I cannot wait to spend more time together—

xoxo
Ali

To all the Rebellious Women who have

transformed their lives through the power

of self investment and self love...

(And some Kick Ass Red Lipstick)

Foreword

Do you dream about your life?

Dreams that make you wonder what you are doing with yourself, and question why you don't have more. Dreams that show you how you could be, if you only had the courage to transform.

Your life might be close to perfect. You may have a job you love and a great relationship. Yet there is something missing, and you just can't put your finger on it. At times, you think about doing something different, just for you...

You might think back to a time when you belonged to something that mattered: maybe a small group of women who did everything together, or a sorority. In your heart, you long for purpose and engagement.

We all sometimes wonder what legacy we are leaving for our loved ones. What will they say about us when we're gone? Did we build something, or bring a group of people together under a cause? Amass a large fortune or write an opus? Did we ever dance on a beach in Spain, or drink wine in Italy?

Of course, our normal answer is to say that we created a family, went to college, started a career or married our sweetheart. These are legitimate legacies. But we are talking about a kind of panic here: the kind of panic where you wake up at 3 a.m., gripping your chest and wondering, "What have I done with my life"?

We believe you are here to do something special. You are on earth to create a wave that enhances your life and expands to affect everyone around you. Our current paradigm limits this wave to a ripple. We can be important, but only within the confines of what society thinks is acceptable for women. Our act of rebellion is drinking a little too much chardonnay while watching a racy TV show. We want to flip that script and make you the star in your own movie; other woman can cry on the couch while watching you stroll the streets of Paris.

We invite you to shift the way you see things. We invite you to see yourself in a new light. We invite you to have that big dream, and to create your life in its own image. We want you to take the slate, the set of expectations you have of yourself, and break it into tiny pieces. We want you to look in the mirror with brave love. We want you to realize that your courage was in your back pocket, this whole time. We want you to cry, to feel the joy of accomplishment welling up from your chest. We want you to cry – but this time, cry because you have found something that you knew you needed.

You are special. You are a wildfire of possibility. You are a dream-maker, a woman of intense possibility and prowess; you just forgot that along the way. As little girls, we knew we would grow up to be something exceptional. We felt in our hearts that we were here on earth to have amazing experiences and to create value. But we forgot what it means to feel special. We forgot what it means to have insane dreams. We traded our desires for comfort, for the safety of a nine-to-five job, a mortgage and credit card debt. But there is a way out.

What comes next will require a leap of faith. It will require you to turn off the part of your brain that says what women can and can't do, and turn on the part that remembers that you are extraordinary, and you are here to do something important. If you can do that, it is my belief that the world will be a better place with you in it.

Chapter One: Trailer Park Swirl

I woke up in the trailer at three in the morning. I could hear every drop of rain landing above my head. I was in a metal house and a storm was playing my roof like a cheap drum. Divorced from a trying marriage, I found myself alone with my two children in a brutal situation.

I knew something was wrong. My senses were fine-tuned... I sat up and listened. Feeling that something was out of place, I got up to check on my kids. I turned on the light in my daughter's room, then checked on my son. I stood there watching him breathe and immediately realized why I had woken.

I heard the front door almost cave in, as though someone was trying to kick it down. I stood, frozen, in the doorway to my son's room, hoping the sound was lightning, a pan falling in the kitchen, or anything other than what I knew it to be.

A man screamed from outside the front door, "Cat! Open this door!"

I turned off the light in my son's room and crouched down, hoping the man wouldn't notice. My breath became measured and I was unsure of what to do next.

What would I do if this man broke into my trailer?

How would I protect my children?

What did he want?

What was he capable of doing?

I was living in a car-crash that was playing out before my eyes.

I moved to the trailer after getting divorced, my only option. I got married too young and made too many compromises along the way. I won't delve too far into what that relationship involved, but it is safe to assume that many of you reading this book have been through similar tragedies. Yet there I was, a single mother of two kids, alone in a trailer park, with a crazy man trying to kick in my flimsy door.

There are points in our lives when everything starts to pivot. There are points within us when we decide that enough is enough and that we will no longer rely on others to survive. There are points when the expectations of our upbringing get tossed out and rebuilt in our own image. There are points when we become us, when we become who we were meant to be, because we have no other choice.

We find ourselves fighting for our lives, in a trailer in the rain, looking at ourselves in the mirror and wondering where we went wrong. We are desperate and alone, doomed to do the same thing over and over until we finally realize that there is something else out there. We are broken physically and emotionally, trampled and demonized. We are put upon to carry the burden of others, mules that bear the weight of other people's self-loathing and delusions. Society expects women to throw themselves into these roles with full conviction. Yet what ends up happening? We completely lose ourselves in the process and end up immersed in drama.

As women, the world can see us as their playthings, their nurse-maids, the objects of their dark fantasies. It is implied that we do the laundry, care for the children, clean the toilets and give up our dreams and desires. As women, we easily drift into a space where we accept those roles. It's a dangerous dichotomy: we are supposed to be sexy for our partners, but we also need to be the custodian, manager, and mother.

Have you had this problem? I have, over and over.

And yet, there comes a point in our lives when we say enough is enough. As I sat there, crouched in my tin-can kitchen, wondering if I was going to have to fight a drunk man as he broke down my door, everything changed.

The man was a neighbor in the trailer park. I had met him once, for less than five minutes. I gave him the wrong idea, obviously. He screamed something unintelligible as my hand slowly opened the kitchen drawer and felt for my dollar-store kitchen knife. All I could find was a small paring knife, but I clutched it like a life-line.

I am not the type of woman to cry at the drop of a hat, but I thought about my eight year old daughter in bed, and my eyes turned molten. I thought about my son. What example was I setting, and I put my hand on my mouth as an angry whimper drifted out.

I looked back on my journey: married right after college, with no idea who I was, who I wanted to be. Where did everything go wrong? I knew you were supposed to find someone, get married, and have kids. So I followed instructions, colored inside the lines. I did what every generation did before me. I went to college to find my "Mrs." degree. Every woman in my family was married by the time they were 22 years old – I was no exception.

I went to church.
I cooked meals.
I was up all night with both kids.
I was a taxi service to both my children and my husband.
I changed all the diapers.

I cleaned the kitchen.
I paid all the bills.
I took care of five dogs and two cats.
I did the laundry.
I did all the shopping.
I cleaned the toilets.
I worked two jobs.
I cleaned the house.
I moved from city to city.
I cleaned his hunting gear.
I did what I understood my female duties to be...
almost everything...
I did what my husband told me to do...
I ran myself to the edge of reality, the law, sanity,
and the safety of myself and my children.
Until finally, I was fed up.

I told him I was done, and I moved out, and got a
divorce. Which brings us to the point in the story
when I was crouched in the kitchen of my trailer,
holding a paring knife.

The man screamed, "God dammit Cat, open the
door! I just want to talk!"
I knew what "talking" meant, and I wasn't having
any part of it.

Have you ever been in a situation as a women
where you are friendly to a man and he takes it the
wrong way? Just because I say "hello" does not
mean you own me, or that you have some right to

obsess over me as though I can save you... I can't save any man. I don't want to save a man. I want a man who has his act together, so we can mutually self-respect.

I know this now, but when I was sitting on the floor in my kitchen, I was trying to work out why this man might have misread my intentions.

Bang, Bang, Bang...!

My son stumbled out of his bedroom, to find me crumpled in the kitchen in the dark. "Mom... what's going on?"

"Nothing baby, let's get you back to bed..."

I took him, tucked him in and shut his door. My jaw tightened, and my mind turned to chrome. I walked to the front door of the trailer and stopped. Everything in my psyche shifted away from the default setting of ex-wife, a women that someone can "have", and toward the mindset of a woman that can create her own reality, toward the woman I wanted to be; from a victim of dip-shits, to a woman who influences millions of women to embrace their sensuality, for its own sake, not for the titillation of men.

In that moment, I became *me*. I became a force, a new fire, a punk-rock version of my mind's eye. I *am*.

I set the knife down on the counter as I walked to the front door. I flung open the door, knocking the neighbor onto his back on the mud in the rain.

I screamed, "What do you want?" I stood there like a warrior goddess of old, protecting the threshold between this man and my children...

He stammered to regain control of his Bud Light-soaked brain.

"I, I, just wanted to talk…"

"So you thought kicking in my door would get me in the mood to speak with you?"

"You don't get to speak to me. You don't get to stand on my doorstep. Don't look at me. Don't even think about me. Stay away from me and my children… You understand?"

He tried to stand,

"Yes… Yes ma'am."

He found his footing in the mud and stood.

"But, I…

I dropped my gaze and realized everything had changed for me. I was no longer an ex-wife, I was no longer what society told me to be, I was not a trailer-park-chick, and I sure as hell was not helpless or worthless. I was a woman and I was going to change this situation for myself and my children, no matter what.

I stepped down from the front door of the trailer, my eyes on fire, and that man turned tail and ran...

Chapter Two: Stage Change

I locked the door and walked back through the trailer in the dark. I checked on my son. I walked across the hall to my daughter's room and crawled into bed with her. I hugged her as the rain played a new song on the roof. A smile drifted onto my face as I knew, in that moment, that everything would be different. I wanted from this point onwards to be an example of what a woman truly is, not what society told me to be.

I woke up the next day and got dressed for work. I took my children to school and went to my job at the insurance company. I sat in my cubicle and dreamt of a new life. I laid the mental groundwork for who I was going to be – the real me. I sat there, in that desk job, and knew that I could be more: for me, for my children, and for those around me. I knew it was time to be true to myself and not be a victim of toxic people or situations. I knew I was meant to be more.

It is easy to look at a success story and to assume that someone went from rock-bottom to thriving overnight. This is generally not the case. For me, it took three years to go from the incident in the trailer park to opening the doors of my dance studio.

And there were stumbles along the way. I got involved with men who were broken, who wanted to dress me up so that I matched the image of me that they had created. Realizing this was a big pivot point: I discovered who I was, by being exposed to this "idea of me". I dated a man who always wanted to take me shopping and buy me expensive jeans. You might be thinking, "Girl, what's wrong with that?" On the surface, there is nothing wrong with a loved one wanting to buy you gifts. Being gracious about accepting gifts and compliments is a valuable life-skill. However, Jason wanted to dress me up to look like the girl he wanted to date. He wanted me to wear jeans with designs on the pockets, featuring sequins and sparkles. If you have ever seen my picture, it's easy to tell that I don't wear sparkle jeans. I have nothing against them or people who wear them; they are simply not my style. So Jason wanted to dress me up like his doll, to suit his idea of what women should wear in order to be attractive to men.

It takes a long time to discover who we are, longer to determine who we want to be with. Through this time I was testing out new relationships and finding out who these men were, and who they saw me to be. Jason didn't love me for me, he loved the idea of me in tight sparkle jeans.

Still I kept coming back to that night in the trailer, and one question kept resurfacing. Who was I meant to be? What was I meant to do with my life?

I looked around at the women who were influencing society and I saw women emulating them, changing themselves into different versions of Barbie, faux movie-starlets, or worse. Many women turn themselves into what they think men want. They turn up their sexuality, increasing breast size, boosting lips, butts, and slimming waists. Many women pose for pictures as though they were enticing men into the bedroom, ignoring their impulses to do something meaningful with themselves.

I don't want to be what a man wants me to be. I don't want to be what society, religion, a job or my family wants me to be. I refuse to be a copy of everyone else. I refuse to allow someone to have that power over me. To tell me I can't have tattoos, blue hair, red lips and wear high heels to the grocery store.

My students and I joke about this. We call a man who is a carbon copy of every other man "a Jason". He wears his hat backwards, is overly cocky, but emotionally inept. He wears long shorts and flip-flops and polo shirts. Jason has lots of bros; Jasons travel in packs. Jason and his bros hoot and holler, think everything they say is hilarious. Jasons absolutely LOVE sports. They played sports in high school and will tell you all about how they could've played professionally, if they hadn't hurt themselves in the big game. Jasons should be considered dangerous when drunk or when watching football or when at the strip club. Know a Jason? Jasons are insecure but overcompensate by being full of ego and are more interested in what you can do for them, than in asking themselves "What can I do for her?"

We call women who are copies of every other woman "a Jennifer". She has bleach-blonde hair and a tiny dog that fits in her bag. She wears expensive everything: jeans, watches, blouses, glasses, purses, and jewelry. Jennifer wears makeup to look like someone else. If you see a Jennifer without makeup, you will be shocked. Jennifer hates all women. She sees them as competition. If you are in a room with a Jennifer, she will immediately size you up and decide if she is going to kill you with her eyes or ignore you. It is rare for Jennifers to travel in packs, but when they do, watch out, as it is an experience you want to avoid. They will nitpick everyone and plot to destroy them. Jennifers collect men, chewing through them like handbags. Jennifer should be considered armed and dangerous at all times.

Disclaimer: Of course, we have nothing against women who happen to be named Jennifer, it was simply the name that was most popular when I was growing up. And besides, when you look at a Jennifer, you know she is a Jennifer...

I knew I didn't want to be a Jennifer and I knew I didn't want to date a Jason.

But who was I meant to be? The idea from the trailer park kept hounding me... I didn't want to transform myself into someone else, I just wanted to become me. People often talk about the power of change. I didn't want change for the sake of change, I wanted to be comfortable in my own skin.

I wanted to be the woman I was once, a long time ago. Sometimes who we are meant to be is influenced by who we were in the past, when we were most actualized. That sounds simple enough, but it can be a brutal process of self-discovery, an awful exercise in auditing life experiences and pulling them out, one by one, until we find a clue that leads us in the right direction. I knew one of my passions was to dance, and that I loved teaching others how to dance. Could I do that again?

I started dancing when I was 10 years old. My mom put me in dance lessons at a local studio and I felt at home right away. I was dancing four days a week, choreographing routines to Michael Jackson's "Off The Wall" in my bedroom and performing them in the studio. I would bring my cassettes to Mrs. Keller's 5th grade class. She had a boom box and she would allow me to do my own dances for the class during breaks and lunch time. This was a time in my life when I felt free to be myself and gave NO FUCKS about what others thought of me. I was being true to myself and feeding my soul.

Until one day... I entered the school talent show as the only dance soloist. I wore a black leotard, white fringe, and black fishnets. I was doing a dance to "Let's Hear it for the Boy" that I learned from the studio. Afterwards, they announced the winners – and I did not win. Two judges approached me telling me that I was the best, but the school had already picked the winners prior to the show.

What?

At this moment, I realized that what others think of you does matter. If you stand out, or you don't care what other people think, you can be punished.

I remember being proud of myself and signing off as "Dancing Queen" on my teacher's get-well card – not because I was cocky, but because I thought what I had was special. My classmates teased me all through high school because I signed my name "Dancing Queen". The fire in my mind was starting to be taken from me. I wasn't allowed to be myself, for fear of being ridiculed.

When I started high school, I was told, "You are very talented, but lack confidence". When I danced, I looked at the ground, afraid to make eye contact with those around me. I was scared to be myself while performing. Afraid of being put down, made fun of, teased for being the "Dancing Queen".

As I went through high school, my confidence started to build; I started to feel like myself. I paid attention to my passion for dancing, and started caring less about what others thought of me. I was Captain of the pom-pom team and a featured senior soloist in the dance concert in my senior year. I was voted Most Valuable Dancer in the dance program. However, my confidence improved to the point where I was told that I was "too sexy" when I danced and I needed to "tone it down".

What?

Too confident, not confident enough, now too confident. No wonder our young women are so confused. We are given so many mixed messages as to who we are supposed to be. It seems we just can't win.

I went to college and did not study dance because, "You just can't make a living dancing". I majored in Liberal Studies and stopped dancing. I accepted that dance was for little girls. I was a grown woman and it was time to do grown-up things. My high school dance teacher told me that I was the biggest waste of talent she had ever seen.

Fast forward: married, two children. My husband asked me to find a job (I was a full-time, stay-at-home mom). He put limitations on when I could work, and what I could do. The discussion of substitute teaching came up. I went to the district's website and stumbled across a JV Dance Coach job at the local high school. I spoke to my husband. He did not believe it would be a good idea, but I did it anyway. I got the job. I started coaching and realized how much I missed making an impact on others and how much I missed dancing. I ended up becoming Head Coach within the year and led the program until we had to move to Iowa.

We moved to Iowa and within a few months of living here, another local high school was looking for a dance coach. This time it was different. I was working a full-time job at an insurance company and didn't believe I had the time to devote to coaching. After a lot of thought, I decided I would make the time. I coached again for another year, only quitting due to my emotionally exhausting divorce. But my fire was reignited: I had to do something about it.

I was thirty-nine, a single mother of two teenagers, working full-time at an insurance company. I couldn't possibly open my own dance studio... could I?

I kept asking myself, who was I meant to be? I didn't think I was meant be in a cubicle at a massive company for fifty hours a week. Working in a cube caused me immeasurable grief and was the opposite of what I believed in, but it fed my family and put a roof over our heads. I was meant to be a mother, and raising those glorious creatures was beyond a blessing. But the fact is, they were teenagers and needing me less and less. I didn't think I needed a man in my life, especially since most of them were "Jasons".

I knew I needed to dance. I needed dance like some women need to paint, garden, play an instrument, or sing. I knew I needed to dance. Was I meant to open a dance studio? I asked myself this and listened to the feelings that came back from my mind, my heart, my body. The idea scared the hell out of me, but I decided the answer was yes, I was meant to open a dance studio. Who was I meant to be? I would go back to what I loved, what I knew about myself and the world from the age of four... I was going home, back to dancing.

An important side-note here at this pivotal moment in the story. I only tell you this because so many women have asked me about my story and I want to let you know that despite the struggles we ALL have, if you open up and become more "you", amazing things can happen. I am a regular gal. So please don't think that I am standing on my soap box and telling you my life just to aggrandize myself. If you ask any of the women in my studio, they will tell you I rarely share my story because it's not about me. It's about you, the woman you were born to be. I am simply using my story to invite you to consider your own. – Respectfully, Cat

Where were we? Ok, yes, I decided to open a dance studio. Mind you, up until this point, my only experience as an entrepreneur was selling Pampered Chef. I did not have a huge pile of cash labeled, "Open Dance Studio" socked away somewhere. I had only just bought my first condo and moved out of the trailer park. Where does one begin when attacking a problem this big?

I decided to break it down into pieces. I wrote a business plan and then attacked. I found a sandwich shop in a retail center near my condo that would serve as a location for the studio. Then I went to a local bank to ask for a loan. This is where it gets weird...

I wanted more than just a dance studio. I wanted to create a place where women could go through the same journey of self-discovery as I was on. I wanted to open a place where women could come in and find out who they were. I wanted to open a dance studio for adult women to reconnect or find their own sense of self, their own sensuality, their own secrets. I decided to make the focus of the studio the art of burlesque.

Burlesque came to popularity in the United States and England in the mid-1880s, featuring comedic acts and women cavorting around in different colored tights. Given that women were expected at the time to dress with a sense of heightened decorum, tights made a splash. Historically, the female portion of burlesque was designed to be suggestive, with women revealing themselves slowly through a series of dance moves. In contemporary times, women like Dita Von Teese have brought the art into the modern lexicon with a sense of class.

The important thing to note is that burlesque is not about turning-on men. Burlesque is not about sex. Burlesque is about connecting with your feminine sensuality. It's about owning who you are, who you were meant to be…it's about loving who you are, not who you might be if you get that big promotion or find the right guy. It's about loving yourself right now and as you love and invest in yourself, you can become that person you were meant to be.

So there I was, working a full time job at an insurance company in Iowa. I needed money to open the studio. I went to the bank and gave them my business plan. Imagine walking into a bank with the word 'farmer' in the name and explaining to them that I wanted to open a burlesque studio. I thought I had a 10% chance of getting the loan. I did my homework and showed up with my ducks in a row. To the bank's credit, they believed in me and I had the seed money for my dream. The bank was adamant that I keep my full time job while opening the studio, which I (thankfully) did.

There were many challenges. I had battles with the landlord, my boss discovered I was opening a business, and for a long time nobody understood my mission. Initially, I had classes with zero students. Some of my classes would have two or three women in them. I was doing everything I could to get people to understand my mission of empowering women through the art of burlesque. I did flash mobs, advertised on social media, and passed out flyers.

I ran out of money and had to go back to the bank and ask for more to pay rent for a few more months. The turning point came in January when people have their New Year's resolutions. I started having classes of six and seven. As time went on, more and more women attended classes. I went back to my business plan and thought more about my idea of forming a troupe, which is a performance group. I took eight of my students and created The *Va Va Voom!* The troupe would allow women an outlet to perform their new craft.

The *Va Va Voom!* would host burlesque shows and spread the word about what we were doing and allow the performers to share their newfound confidence.

What happened next surprised everyone. Most of the Midwest is a conservative population masquerading as democrats. Yet one of the largest populations of lesbian women in the United States is thirty minutes from my studio. Somehow, we ended up selling out our first show, packing the house of around 300 seats. Our performances feature choreographed routines set to dance and comedic riot festivals, showcasing women dressed up as lumberjacks, females masquerading as men, and hamburgers being pulled from shorts.

Following that show, the studio, Vitality Fitness and Dance in Cedar Rapids, expanded dramatically. We have helped women get in touch with their inner dancers, teaching everything from burlesque to Vixen Dance fitness classes. But dance is just the hook. Once a woman comes to class and sees there is a place, a culture that gives women permission to be their best selves, things really begin to change.

I am not one of those women who cries at the drop of a hat. I do not cry when I break a nail or have a flat tire. I don't cry when someone yells at me or when I am late for a meeting. When I do find myself in tears, it's because of these women. They come to the studio, broken and bruised, ravaged by men, money, loss, and drama. They come thinking that a class in burlesque would be fun, and they leave realizing that there is a framework in place that allows them to have a new look at who they could be, who they were meant to be.

So I cry when they tell me how their lives change after joining the studio. I cry when they tell me that they have dumped their loser boyfriends and have signed up to return to college. I cry when they tell me that their husbands were initially afraid of them attending classes and now they say, "Whatever you are doing, keep doing it, because you are happy and healthy." I cry when a student tells me she walks five miles to class, because it is that important.

The truth is, as women, we need permission to take the first step toward reclaiming who we were meant to be. We need to know that we aren't selfish, that it's OK to do something just for us, just this once. We need to know that dancing and dreaming is not a sin. We were meant to enjoy this life. We need to know there that were are groups of women out there who are open and brave, who will take us in, and help us along the way. We need permission.

I give you permission. I give you permission to drift back and see who you were before all the compromises. I give you permission to stand in your heart and dream again, to dream of who you could be, outside the cubicles and the confines of debt and daily life. I give you permission to grab yourself, that person you wanted to be, pick yourself up, and hug yourself. I want you to come and stand with us.

Sometimes this is all it takes to set off an avalanche of self-love. Change is a single act of bravery. Sometimes all it takes is to do one thing for yourself. That one thing reminds you that you are a powerful creature, that your life is going to return to your control. Sometimes you have to dance for you, not for anyone else. Sometimes you have to do something just because it makes you feel pretty and to hell with everyone else.

Sometimes, that act of bravery can be as simple as putting on a Kick Ass Red Lipstick.

Chapter Three: The Moment of Truth

He would scream at me, "What the #(&*$ are you putting on lipstick for?"

"…Because I want to feel pretty. I like wearing lipstick."

"Why do you only put on lipstick when you go out…? Are you having an affair?"

"Don't be ridiculous."

"You never wear lipstick for me…"

"I don't wear lipstick for anyone, but me…"

This would throw him further into a fit.

Kick Ass Red Lipstick was born all those years ago, as an angry man tried to blame me for doing something for myself.

And that's the trick. We are tricked into believing that we are supposed to be pretty for other people, that we are supposed to dress in certain ways to attract men. We are tricked into believing that we have to conform to common beliefs about how women should behave.

We are told how to dress, act, and groom at different stages of our lives. If you are a mother of three kids and drive a mini-van, you should have short hair. If you work in a cubicle, your uniform is jeans and frumpy sweatshirts. If you work for an insurance agency, you can wear clothes that can also be worn to church. If you are a Jennifer, you must dress and act like a Jennifer (or Jason will be furious).

This is where Kick Ass Red Lipstick comes in...

We take all that shit and *throw it out the window*. We agree to take one simple step, one brave action, toward becoming who we want to be. We agree to put on lipstick for us.

Kick Ass Red Lipstick is a fire in the dark, a group of women who say, "enough is enough... I'm doing something for me RIGHT NOW". That small action is a symbolic shift that occurs in our lives when we stop existing for the sake of others and put ourselves at the front (or near the front) of the line. Kick Ass Red Lipstick is a reason for us to stand together. It's a rope to pull the dreamers out of the cubicle, to pull the single mothers up from the muck of their reality. Kick Ass Red Lipstick is the key that opens your lock, it's a door to ten thousand more doors...

I ask you to join us. I ask you to come and stand with us, valiantly defying convention. I ask you to put on your rebel panties and step out of your box and rough it up a bit...

Lipstick has a long history wrapped in controversy. The Romans used it to indicate social rank, with both men and women wearing lip-tint. The English attempted to ban the use of lipstick in the 1600s, calling its use a vice. In the early 1900s, leaders of the group promoting women's rights to vote wore bright red lipstick as a sign of solidarity.

You know what women say about bright red lipstick. Someone very close to me told me, "Only sluts wear bright red..." I thought about this for a long time, wondering what year this was, and where are all these sluts hanging around with bright red lipstick? This is a grade-school approach to a modern issue. When we were fourteen, we called girls sluts as a way to pigeon-hole them, as a way to make it acceptable to be bitchy to them. Maybe we wanted to be like them? Do you honestly know any SLUTS? Have you seen a pack of sluts roaming around in red lipstick? I invite you to allow lipstick to open your eyes to what's real and what's driven by male-centric, 1920s thinking.

So in the context of our rebel alliance, what is the purpose of putting on lipstick? I can hear you second-wave feminists grousing about pandering to men's desires by rouging the lips, thereby sending a sign that you are 'available'. I can hear the nature girls saying that putting on lipstick is just a way to cover up who you are.

The purpose is to self-engage, to invest, if only for a moment, in thinking of just you. The purpose is to remember what it's like to feel pretty. Our sensual natures do not belong to advertising agencies, or locked away by some male-driven-dogma. The act of applying lipstick is a sign to yourself that you own your own sense of sensuality, outside of any relationship. It is a sign to the world that you are bravely stepping out.

Do you remember what it was like to be a young girl, playing with your mother's lipstick, digging in her purse to find her favorite shade and sneaking off to apply it in the bathroom? You felt powerful, an odd sense of sophistication washed over you. You weren't telling the world you were ready to date, you weren't putting it on for a man, you were a rebel. You were grasping the power of *you* for one of the first times. You were finding the power in a Kick Ass Red Lipstick.

So if that's the power of lipstick, what's the point of the Kick Ass Red Lipstick group? To put it simply, raucous engagement. We take a bunch of women who have done what was expected of them for the last ten to fifty years, invite them to throw on some lipstick and step out with us. Who knows what will happen when like-minded women gather together with the same thoughts of being lost and not knowing who they are anymore? The purpose is to bond with women just like you: cubicle warriors, waitresses (especially the genius kind), expended mothers, executives with souls worn thin, students who know stuff but want to know real stuff, divorced and dramatized survivors, and all. Give yourself to us and we will give you back to you…

Disclaimer: While we say that we are a bunch of rebels (which is true), to put a finer point on it, this is not a pack of drunken, lip-swollen hussies. We are classy gals, putting on our best dresses and going out to meet some like-minded ass-kickers.

'So how do I join Kick Ass Red Lipstick?'

Simple: find a Kick Ass Red Lipstick and apply it to your lips. Sit back and observe the change. For extra points, post your selfie on our social groups, along with the flocks of other brave women. This is the first and most important mission: apply kick ass red lipstick.

Here are the steps:

1. Find a shade. This is simple, yet complex. The key is to find something a bit redder, a step outside of your comfort zone. Red is our recommendation, but you could also go with purple, black, nude, or anything fancy. We find many women saying, 'I don't wear lipstick, so here is a selfie of me wearing lip balm…' or "Red works for other women, not me". Sorry

ladies, this is not an excuse. There are blue-reds and yellow-reds that fit with every skin tone. Take your girlfriend and go to your local cosmetic store and start sampling the different shades of red you can get your hands on. Remember, this group is called, Kick Ass Red Lipstick, not Super Duper ChapStick or the "I Don't Believe In Makeup" Society. You must put on some lipstick. It's the pivot between ChapStick and transformation. You can start with nude shades, if you need to work into the process (more on how to do this later).

2. Observe. Look in the mirror. See yourself as a new woman. See yourself as empowered. See yourself doing something you have always wanted to do. See yourself leading a group of women, taking that road trip, or creating art. Watch how people interact with you in a different way. You will find yourself walking taller. Trying on that dress you have always wanted. Getting a babysitter for the first time and having a ladies night out. Buying those heels you have been eying for a long time but never bought because "I have nowhere to wear them". Well, now you do. You can wear them with your Kick Ass Red Lipstick. Watch the change. Feel the love.

3. Engage. Use your social tools to open the door to other women who could benefit from

lipstick, just like you. The women who are afraid to take that step. The women who have been lost for a long time and don't know where to turn. The ones who need "permission" to be themselves and finally start loving who they are. Create a local chapter and inspire yourself and others...

Chapter Four: Quintessence

You may have heard of Norma Jeane Mortensen. She started off with the last name Mortensen, but ended up taking her mother's maiden name of Monroe and the first name of her favorite film actress, Marilyn Miller. We know her as Marilyn Monroe, and her name is part of her power, part of her charm. Nothing wrong with being a Mortensen, but there is power in taking on an alter-ego.

So we invite you to play with Quintessence. What does that mean? According to the dictionary, it is "the pure and concentrated essence of a substance. Or the most perfect embodiment of something". Look at your life and create yourself an avatar, a quintessential expression of who you envision yourself to be.

At my dance studio, students are encouraged to come up with an alter-ego, a way of understanding themselves from another point of view, an escape from their lives as Jennifer, to become what they were meant to be. This process can be difficult, getting free reign is not something we are equipped to handle. Permission to be free is not something we understand. We think there is freedom in money, in good jobs and fancy cars, but true freedom, the rip-roaring, blazing explosion on the edge of the nighttime in our souls, is accepting that you can create yourself in whatever way you want, that you can stop, right now, being that thin-brained, life-administrator and throw down a new gauntlet, toss out your victim and go dancing in a red dress with that woman you were meant to be. Give her a name, and kick open the door to your new life, hair on fire, metaphorical motorcycle skidding out of the parking lot...

So I give you permission. I am standing at the door, inviting you in...

I give you permission to create yourself in the way you want to be. I give you permission to wear Kick Ass Red Lipstick and to look yourself in the mirror and see who you are. The catharsis, the change moment, is pushing your boundary to wear something you wouldn't normally wear, on one of the most intimate parts of your body, your lips. Once you dive into that new pool, you have taken your first steps toward true freedom. And not freedom as it relates to governmental control, or financial freedom, or freedom of expression, but the freedom we can all generate, the incendiary mind-bomb that allows you to see everything from a new vantage point.

Create yourself: I dare you.

Important note: When creating one's new self, it is critical to understand our motivations. For me, I want to be empowered, it's who I am. It's critical not to create an alter ego that is broken or pushes you into the category of perpetual victim (or keeps you there). I see so many women who have a princess complex, it's an actual tragedy. (Jennifer anyone?)

When we were little girls, we had dolls and princess dresses and Barbies and bullshit that anchored our expectations in a realm that is dangerous and the opposite of empowering. If you grow up and marry someone who adores you and treats you like a princess, excellent. But in general, life doesn't work that way. You are not a princess at the DMV, you are not a princess at your child's school play, you are not a princess according to the IRS, you are not a princess when you are being a bitch because you feel you are prettier than "her". Installing or perpetuating this myth is worse than smoking meth while flying an airplane. Do not give yourself a princess persona. It is a slippery slope my dears. There is a difference between being on a "power trip" and being "empowered". Princesses are on a continuous "power trip". Princesses do not find happiness from within – they look to others to make them happy. They usually don't want other women around. Princesses want women to know that they are better than everyone else. Princesses are the type of women that claim they "don't get along with other women". I wonder why? They may claim that they have self-love and support women but the fact is, they don't. They think they understand what being empowered is, but they have an unrealistic expectation of how they are to be treated and what being empowered is really about. Believe me, I have seen it happen. If you have a princess complex, you should consider killing that part of you, right now.

Romantic comedies are a pox on women for this very reason. Two people who don't belong together fall in love, there is a huge problem in one of their lives, they break up, he chases her around, against all odds, he finds a way to convince her that she is the greatest thing ever and they ride off into the sunset. See every romcom… ever…and this puts us in the princess panties again, assuming that a person is going to ride in and save us from ourselves or our circumstances. Strong women are not dollies and do not play with doll versions of themselves in their heads.

So be free, but don't be free to pretend you are a dolly. You are not a princess. You do not need saving. You are not here to find happiness in others. You are here to find the happiness in yourself.

You are a stunning piece of moving art, a shifting wave of possibilities, a superhero, guardian, a lover, sexy dreamer. Create your reality in your own image, not based on bullshit and Barbies.

Here are the steps:

1. Remember. Who did you want to be when you were younger? I don't care if you wanted to be a princess (see above). Think about a time when you were a bit older than that... Who did you want to be when you were twelve? Did you want to be a ballerina, a doctor, a lawyer, a mother? What do all those things have in common? They are power positions that allow for tangible impact on lives. You did not want to be a cubicle jockey. You did not want to be a waitress. You did not want to get your boyfriend a beer while he watches six hours of football every weekend while you starve for his attention.

2. Dream. Creating an alter-ego is a tough process that may take some time to accomplish (and change is allowed). What do you want? Who do you want in your life? What would create a sense of purpose and engagement? What would make you feel special when you show up to a meeting of Kick Ass Red Lipstick? I challenge you to buy a journal that reflects you and start writing down what you are looking for. One of the students who attends my studio claimed she came to class because it made her "interesting". What would

make you interesting? Working at the kids' taco stand or volunteering for the company Christmas party isn't exactly categorized as interesting.

3. Sketch. Get a piece of paper or make notes on your phone of names of people who inspire you. Oprah, Madonna, Kat Von D... Google 'movie-star name generator' or 'super hero name generator' and play around with different combinations. Maybe you had a nickname when you were younger and felt more empowered. Maybe you empathize with Foxy Brown from the 70s or your crazy art teacher or a comedian from college... Maybe you name yourself after your favorite shade of lipstick? For example: Dissolved in Dreams or Truffle Tease? You are free to create you. Put things together, mix it up. Post your new alter-ego on one of our social sites. Bam, new you!

Chapter Five: Lipstick Legacy

We create a legacy with every moment we spend on earth. Some of us will leave a wealth of money, children, buildings, art, cars, and homes. Others will create vast banks of experiences, preferring to explore life by banging into the guardrails, pushing themselves and creating expansive adventures. Flocks of women leave a legacy of survival, fighting war and poverty; digging with everything they have just to get clean water for their families. Other women will leave a legacy of destruction, exploded by alcohol, drug abuse, and self-pity.

There is no correct way to live your life. But one thing is abundantly clear: those of us who have the opportunity to create amazing life experiences, we owe it to the women who fight for their lives to create something positive. One of our missions at Kick Ass Red Lipstick is to create a framework for women to become conscious of their legacy and to give them a path to create what they want with their lives.

As you know, as women, we are excellent at making other people's focus our own and end up living the lives of people who surround us: husbands, boyfriends, children, celebrities. We put ourselves on the back-burner, sometimes for life. We give up what we want so our husband can get an M.B.A. We work two jobs so our kids can go to the best schools. We drive junky cars so our husbands can go hunting and fishing with the boys. We cook dinner and do the dishes, after working the exact same amount of time as our spouses.

It isn't your fault. We are taught this from early childhood. We are selfish if we don't give our marriage, our children, and our job everything. If we self-invest, others judge us. "Can you believe she is at yoga during her kid's basketball practice?" It's not just others who judge us – it's other women. Women are horrible to other women. Women are always in competition to see who is the best cook, best mom, best spouse, or the best breadwinner. If you don't drive your kids to five different activities a week, or volunteer for the PTA or prepare all the meals for family…there is something wrong with you. Ladies…what the fuck?

Women are scared to self-invest and judge women who do. Women are threatened when they see a woman love herself. Why? Why don't you want to love you? How do you expect other people to love you and give you respect if you don't do those things for yourself? If you met yourself today at a party, what would you say to yourself?

We do nothing for ourselves. If we even CONSIDER doing something nice for ourselves, we are immediately selfish witches. We are professionals at giving up on ourselves.

That stops now. We command you to do something for yourself. We command you to encourage other women to do something for themselves. Truth be told, you are already doing something for yourself. You are reading this book. You are taking a bold step, a leap of faith toward the next exceptional chapter in your life...

Let me introduce you to the Kiss List, a path of personal expansion. What's the Kiss List? It's a ladder for you to get to where you want to be. It's a legacy tool, a dream exposure device, a crowbar under your life. The Kiss List is a trail of breadcrumbs you leave for the people in your life so they can follow you into the wilderness. The Kiss List is you, without all the bullshit you make up about yourself.

So how does it work?

The Kiss List is a game, a game of life. How do you play? Read on.

Chapter Six: Part One: Blushing Pink

Often we see women come to us wearing no lipstick and declaring that they will never wear lipstick. That's fine, but this group is called Kick Ass Red Lipstick. In order to be a member, you must wear lipstick of some color. Relax. We aren't asking you to run naked through downtown. It's just color on your lips. If you don't want to wear lipstick, go join your local hiking group or a group for cross-stitch. But don't give us grief about not wearing lipstick. Read the label… It says, "Kick Ass Red Lipstick". If you don't want to play, don't get mad at us because you ignored the label or thought it didn't apply to you.

Women who resist the idea often start with a pink or a nude lipstick. We see a dramatic change in a woman as she grows through these shades, from pink to crimson and beyond. It's a process, a journey from seeing yourself as you do now, to moving through the world in another way altogether. It's part of who we are, we transform women from wallflowers to ass-kickers.

One does not simply decline to wear lipstick and show up at one of our gatherings. Lipstick required. However, we are understanding of the process of going from nothing, to nude, to pink, to rouge, to crimson. As such, we have built our organization to track these changes.

Each process has a corresponding lipstick shade:

- The first part of the process is Blushing Pink.

- The second part of the process is Rebel Rouge.

- The third is Vixen Scarlet.

As you move through the process and join us in Kick Ass Red Lipstick, you gain recognition for your accomplishments and get to help other women.

Let's review: In order to join Kick Ass Red Lipstick, all you have to do is take a picture of you wearing a Kick Ass Red Lipstick. In the second step in Kick Ass Red Lipstick, we encourage women to create an alter-ego, an avatar of themselves using Quintessence. The third step is taking the journey through what we call the "Kiss List".

Most of us have experienced set-backs, some loss that left us feeling less feminine, less sensual, less whole. As women, we have shouldered vast responsibility, taken care of children, jobs, businesses, aging parents, not to mention adult-man-children. A lot of us have fallen into a state where we see ourselves in a subservient role within our relationships. We do everything, and I mean everything, for other people. We shop, we work, we cook, we do the dishes, we pay the bills, we clean the house, we make sure the oil is changed in the cars, we take the kids to and from school, we make lunches, we make sure our parents are well... we do it all.

What we don't do is take care of ourselves. We do nothing for ourselves, but perhaps indulge in shitty television, over-eat fake food, and maybe go to a dank gym to counter the two previous splurges. We are not in love with ourselves, partially due to the fact that we do nothing for ourselves. You ignore yourself at every turn, give yourself away for nothing, no thanks, or worse.

Think about it. How many times do you work a nine hour day, come home, cook a meal, and your kids and your spouse push away from the table and disappear, no thanks, no help with the dishes, no nothing? It's like you are the waitress, the cook, the dishwasher, and the maid. And the funny thing is you are doing this to you.

One: You allow it. A Kick Ass Red Lipstick Society member has every right to take all the dirty dishes from dinner and put them on her kid's beds. You have every right to establish a new rule. "Whoever cooks, does not clean". This is just one example. Think of how many tiny tragedies you agree to. Does your husband think it's funny if he makes fun of the way you look, walk, or talk?

Two: You do nothing for yourself. Nothing. Zero, zip, nada.

How could you love someone who treats you the way you treat yourself? Impossible (or at least not healthy). You do nothing for you. You don't love yourself and part of the reason is you treat yourself like shit. This is an important concept. You can say you love yourself all you want, but if you treat someone you love with disdain, the relationship will fail, leaving you alone, in a room with yourself, perpetrator of damage by lack of attention.

Not inspired. Not taken care of. Not embraced.

But you do things for everyone else in your life. Does that make sense? Does that engender a bit of resentment on your part? You wouldn't ever verbalize this, but if you give and give and give, do nothing for yourself and get nothing in return, it's natural to feel like you are being taken for granted. This leads to all sorts of issues, like divorce, substance abuse, and a general feeling of low self-esteem and lack of confidence.

Solution? The first section of the Kiss List: Blushing Pink.

Pink has a bad name, helped along by awful holiday cards, slogans on ass cheeks, and some aberration called "hot pink". Have no fear... We are here to rescue pink, to bring it back from the brink, to refresh its blushing beauty. Our pink is the color of pearls who have been out too late. Our pink is the color of a cherry blossom rain. Our pink is inspired by flower petals that have been dipped in the dreams of you, the moment before a perfect kiss.

Our first color, Blushing Pink, is where we start on the Kiss List. This process of growth, this process of moving through Kick Ass Red Lipstick, begins here.

The first thing you need is something to write on. Remember the journal we asked you to get when you were determining your alter-ego? Grab it now, find a quiet space, and take a seat.

Your first assignment is to write down a list of small things you could do for yourself. They should be small, like getting a manicure or buying a new Kick Ass Red Lipstick. Maybe buy a new pair of panties. The objective is to set small, yet achievable goals for yourself, to stair-step from your current level of self-investment, which if you are like most women, is close to zero, to the first step, a tiny butterfly-kiss to remind you that you are alive, that there is someone, at least one person, who loves you dearly…and that person will be you.

Write down at least five items. Once you have these items on your Kiss List, make a plan to accomplish one thing from your list immediately, or sooner. This sounds easy, but you may discover some resistance.

- You may be a wife in a relationship that doesn't allow for self-expression, hampered by extreme budgeting, or jealous insanity.

- You might be a college student who can't see the benefit of carving out an hour to go do something for yourself.

- You might be a single mother of two, working a full-time job, and can't imagine being able to get away for a small amount of time for yourself.

- You are afraid of being judged by others because this is the first time in a long time you have done something just for you.

There are a million reasons that you can't take on the first challenge on our Kiss List. There are a million reasons not to change. The status quo, even if it is a hell-bound, meta-nightmare, is familiar, safe-ish. But if you kick in your door and rescue yourself, you can come and stand with us, on the other side, a throng of super women, infused with guts and grace.

Remember that sign in the airplane that tells you to put the oxygen on your own face first, so that you can help those around you without dying...?

This moment, is that sign, for your life.

How do you benefit from Blushing Pink? What are the benefits of running off to the nail salon? Could it be that you can mark a tiny win in your favor? Could it be that you can look at your nails again and dream of that girl you wanted to be? Could it be that you can pull out your wallet and instead of buying something for your family, you buy something for yourself, you buy a tiny indulgence, a firecracker in the darkness of life?

We think it is important to share this gesture with someone. Call your sister or your gal-pal from college. Post your achievement on one of our social groups. Let people know that you give a shit about yourself. Let yourself know you care.

As I mentioned, the Kiss List, this tiered set of games, is three-fold. Blushing Pink is the first of the three. As with the stages of life, we start out in Blushing Pink and end up in Vixen Scarlet.

Once a woman does a minimum of ten things for herself, from her Blushing Pink Kiss List, we call her a "Blushette". The Blushettes are a group of blooming women, learning to take care of themselves, to put themselves first. Blushettes get together to help each other. Blushettes, bring new women to Kick Ass Red Lipstick so that the message of empowerment and self-investment spreads, one pair of lips at a time.

Once you become a Blushette, you are eligible to wear the Blushette Pin, a symbol that you are an Official Blushette. Wear it with pride.

So you have your first Kiss List Journey: Write down a list of small things you can do for yourself. Then go and do a minimum of ten. Don't forget to revisit this list in the future if you get caught up in the day-to-day drama of over-indulging in other people's needs. There is no timeline when this list needs to be completed. Being a busy woman myself, I understand the time constraints we go through. However, remember this list is important to YOU. I highly encourage you to do at least one item a week.

Do not skip Blushing Pink. This step is crucial to your accomplishment of the subsequent Journeys in this book.

Examples of Blushette List:

- Get your nails done.

- Buy yourself some new sharp kitchen knives.

- Go buy some cheap costume jewelry at the dollar store or a vintage store. I used to do this all the time when I was living in the trailer. It's a great way to accessorize and feel beautiful on a budget.

- Buy and wear fake eyelashes.

- Take a piece of chalk and color a stripe in your hair. "Chalk is cheap!"

- Get your ears pierced.

- Get a canvas (or paper) from the craft store and some dollar paints and brushes. PAINT!

- Get a massage (maybe from local beauty school).

- Buy a set of matching bra and underwear.

- Buy a nice set of pajamas.

- Go buy your most favorite perfume or coffee.

- Go to the movies or a restaurant by yourself.

- Plant the flowers you have always wanted to plant. Buy a houseplant or a goldfish.

- Get a tiny tattoo.

Chapter Seven: Rebel Rouge

This next bit is where the water gets a bit deeper, but don't be scared. We are here for you.

In the first part of the Kiss List, we learned that most women come through this process, a bit shy, unable to connect immediately with a deep red lipstick. So we walk women through the process, a shade at a time. The next step (or lipstick color) in the process is called Rebel Rouge and we call women in this step the "Rebels". This process is list-driven once more, calling you to create things that are important to you and then accomplish them, one by one.

After you accomplish Part One, sit down and think about fun. I don't mean think about what makes you happy; this time, I want you think about what's fun for you. What do you like to do? Write these things down. Do you like sailing? Do you like eating at fancy restaurants? Do you like shopping for vintage clothes? Do you love makeup? Do you like blowing glass? Do you like dancing, learning new languages, going on road trips, or drinking high-end whiskey?

These should be bigger items than your Blushette ideas. These are not trivial journeys. They should be big enough for you to be surprised by some of your approaches. They don't have to be expensive, but if you have money, don't feel like you have to pretend you don't. What is fun to you?

DO NOT SAY, "I like running". You might like running and it might be fun for you. You might get lots of joy from exercise. We understand, it's critical. However, we are not looking for maintenance items. We don't care that you like cleaning your garage…We want to know what you want to do that you consider genuine fun.

Dig into what you like to do. DO NOT SAY, "I love spending time with my kids." Fuck, we know that! The 'I am a martyr' lists will get torn to shreds. DO NOT SAY ANY BULLSHIT about what you do for other people or in your roles as mother, employee, boss, wife, girlfriend or ANYONE else.

What is fun? It is something that sets your hair on fire. It is a rebel note to the world about who you are as a human, a woman, a lover of self. Fun is over and above what we are normally expected to do. Fun is a raucous remembrance of who we were going to be when we were girls. Fun is doing something amazing, for you and your gal-pals. Fun is a little bit outlaw. Not outlaw in the way that biker gangs are outlaws. Fun is a little bit tawdry, a little bit taboo, but not dirty. Fun is doing the things you have always wanted to do. Fun is that thing you look back on, when you are much older and laugh about, the thing you tell your grandkids about and they don't believe you.

What is NOT fun (for our purposes)? Some of these things might be fun, but we want stuff that will turn on your mental lights:

- Watching TV is not fun.

- Mowing the lawn or pulling weeds is not fun.

- Cleaning your basement is not fun.

- Taking things to donate is not fun (it might make you feel good, but what we want is HAIR ON FIRE FUN).

- Going to the container store to organize your garage is not fun.

- Going to networking events is not fun.

- Cooking a new recipe for your family is not fun.

- Making sure you drink 8 glasses of water a day is not fun.

- Buying a new set of dishtowels and matching kitchen curtains is not fun.

Spending time with your kids is fun. They are your children, I understand. However, doing things for your kids or your spouse is not what we are talking about. Kids' activities in any form are not to be included on this list. As I tell my students all the time, YOU were YOU before your spouse or kids came along. What would that person think was fun? It's time to feed the gal who has always been there but has been neglected in so many ways.

Your spouse is self-invested. They go golfing, hunting, and they meet their friends for Happy Hour after work. If they want something new, they go and buy it. You always say "yes" when they ask if they can self-invest. If you were your own spouse, would you give yourself permission to have fun? If someone asked your spouse what you did for fun, how would they respond?

Your children are self-invested. They are involved with activities that you have given them permission to do. What do your teenagers do on a Friday or Saturday night? They go and do things with their friends...doing the things they love to do. Ladies, your children live by example. If you asked your kids what they thought their mom did for "fun", what would the answer be?

Write down a list of *at least* ten things that are fun for you. Read the list. How do you feel when you think about each item?

How would it feel to take an impromptu road trip? How would it feel to stay up all night and watch the sun come up from your roof? How would it feel to go sailing again, just like you did when you were a little girl? How about taking those classes you have always wanted to take but were afraid of having too much fun? Burlesque anyone?

Part of knowing ourselves is knowing what we consider fun. Next time you have free time, reference this list, then go do it! Next time you want something to look forward to, pull out your Rebel Rouge Kiss List, and pick something fun!

I challenge you to accomplish one of these items in the next five days. I double-dog-dare you to accomplish one of these items in the next thirty-six hours.

Action is a drug. Take it.

In the Blushing Pink chapter, we said that in order to become a Blushette, you needed to accomplish ten things from your Blushing Kiss list in order to be known as a Blushette. In this chapter, Rebel Rouge, we want you to do to five items off your Rebel Kiss List to earn the title of Rebel. Tough assignment, we know... Go have fun. Once you have accomplished five items on your Rebel List, check in with our team and we will send you the Rebel Pin!

This portion of your transformation encourages you to align with your inner Rebel. Let's take a moment to define what we mean when we say

Rebel, as the word comes loaded with all sorts of connotations. To us, a Rebel is the new lioness, a leader among women, a flame reignited that lights a million more fires. To us, a Rebel is not someone who acts like a teenage girl. We are classy, sophisticated, empowered, beautiful women. To us, a Rebel is a shocking fun lever, a pivotal surly grandmother, a shout in the dark.

Most of our world is covered with followers, who just do what they are told. Most of the world has no fun. Most of the world has no idea what is fun for them. Most of our world is boring and dreamless. Most of our time is spent falling down, time and again. We experience so much pain and heartache. We do what needs to be done, just to be able to survive – to be warriors.

As a Rebel, we brush that stuff off and start anew. We emerge, as women who embrace the temptation of falling in love with ourselves again. We lean into our hearts, pulling dangerous secrets out, dusting them off and letting them drift off towards the moon. As Rebels, we take back the world. As Rebels, we become the color of our lipstick, stepping out into a new framework, where we are in charge...

Part of our responsibility as Rebels is to show other women the path. Part of our responsibility as the raucous outlaws is to whisper in the ear of other women and say, "over here, we have something for you..." As such, in order to be a true Rebel, get out there and post pictures of you doing items off you Rebel List. Post your Rebel Pin. Post your new adventure land. Post pictures of you becoming a Rebel, so other women can be drawn into your flow.

One of my mantras: I give you permission to be your best self.

It's time for *you* to give women "permission" to self-invest – to be true to themselves.

Examples of Rebel List:

- Get a group of women together and have a picnic in a weird place: on a boat dock, in a snow covered park, on top of a skyscraper. Just think – all it takes is a card table, red lipstick, a beautiful table cloth, and some cheese and wine.

- Take a friend and some basic tools to the junkyard and come back with a hood ornament or something fun. Kick a dented car door. Create something that reflects who you are.

- Go to the local Goodwill or Salvation Army and pick some random clothing items and design your own outfit.

- Freestyle: Get in your car with some gals and drive to a town near to you. Find a hotel that appeals to you and walk in and ask them for a room. Take yourself to dinner and enjoy.

- Learn the language you have always wanted to learn.

- Get a bunch of your lipstick gals together, stack a bunch of wood in a pile and set it on fire.

- Learn to drive a race car (on ice?).

- Take the train somewhere awesome. Amtrak has routes all over the country. Get a posse together and take the overnight train to nowhere.

- Take a red lipstick photo in a place of power that belongs to a group that opposes women. Think: gun shop, taxidermist, sports bar, football stadium, etc.

- Leave kiss marks in weird spots like on the airplane window or mirror in the bathroom.

- Know that restaurant you have been dying to try but no one will go with you? It's time to experience it for yourself. As empowered women we don't need to have a dinner date. All you need is your sassy-self and your Kick Ass Red Lipstick. Be an example to those women who are afraid to step outside the box. You would be surprised how much you learn about yourself by being your own dinner date and meeting total strangers on your own.

Chapter Eight: Prelude to a Vixen

It's wise at this juncture to stop and take a break, before we get too deep. It's important to note that Jennifers (and Jasons, for that matter) will look at this process and think what they are programmed to do: if I don't do it, it is obviously stupid.

Don't be influenced by dummies. Use your own brain. What is Kick Ass Red Lipstick, really? Is it bad? It's a group of women getting together and bettering themselves, for them, for a change. If that's bad, I don't want to be good.

Embrace the Rebel in you.

Part of this process can be seen as a psychological room-cleaning. Go through your friend list and boot everyone who causes you drama, even if you have known them since you were ten. Give this book to everyone who might benefit. If they refuse to read and they're still stuck, get rid of them. Life is too short to deal with bitchy Jennifers. Women who are self-invested and support women with the same mantra are a threat to those who don't understand. If they don't want to be a part of your new-found sisterhood, that's alright. As long as you get encouragement and positivity from your friends on your journey, they are worth being a part of your life. The others? They can go on their own journey of jealousy, judgment, misunderstanding and insecurity. They can continue on their way claiming they "don't have any girlfriends", and you can understand why.

Back to the fun stuff…

Chapter Nine: Vixen Scarlet

So let's review. We start out by taking a picture wearing a Kick Ass Red Lipstick. Then we create our alter-ego with Quintessence. Then we enter our journey, becoming Blushettes and then Rebels. The next portion of our adventure is one of the most challenging, one that might pull you into a realm with fewer shadows, a place where you can be you, the real you, the one you have always wanted to be. Welcome to the next shade, Vixen Scarlet.

We move from Blushing Pink, a brilliant new change in the way we see ourselves, to Rebel Rouge, an expansion in our ability to feel like a person, to be actualized, into our third step: Vixen Scarlet.

What is your legacy? What do you want to be remembered for doing? Think well into the future. Will your great-great-great-grandchildren know who you are, or will you be a passage online: "Sara M., Administrative Assistant, mother of two"?

Our legacy can be manifold. We can be known as a world traveler, an adventure seeker, or an outlaw. We can be known as a writer, speaker, dreamer. Part of our legacy is what we do next. What will our big ideas be? What do we want?

We know what to do to self-invest and what we can do to have fun. Now, we want to know what your big ticket items are... What do you want to do with the time you have left on earth? Do you want to spend some of it inspiring other women? Maybe you want to start your own Lipstick Society Chapter? Maybe you have always wanted to travel around the world?

Write down a list of big-ticket items you want to accomplish before you die. Don't edit yourself. If you want to walk from New York to Florida, write it down. If you want to build a monument to your grandmother, write it down. If you want to walk behind a waterfall, write it down. Eat Belgium waffles in Belgium? Run a marathon wearing lipstick? See a volcano? Sleep on the beach? Have a food fight? Dive with whales? Skydiving? Rope swing? Leaning Tower of Pisa picture? Walkabout in Australia? Tea ceremony in Japan? Sailing cruise in Mediterranean? Zip-line through the jungle? Sleep in a tree-house? Float in the Dead Sea? Hike the Grand Canyon? Igloo in Iceland? Swim with sharks? Learn to surf? Ice skate in New York City? Visit every country in the world? Write a novel? Open your own business? Drive from New York to Los Angeles?

Humans have achieved great things. We have built metal birds to fly across oceans, constructed pyramids, and changed the course of nations. I challenge you to expand your reach into the realm of something that would shock you. Expand your reach into something that makes your nose bleed, it is so far out in the atmosphere that you can not only change you own life, but it can affect the way all women exist in the world. Want to stop terrorism? Create a philosophy that brings all women together, all over the world. Want to stop hunger? Work with technologists to leverage new ideas to bring clean water and food to millions, using the power of women. Want to inspire a generation? Help bring Kick Ass Red Lipstick to a legion of women, changing the way they feel about themselves and how they interact.

This list should not contain copies of items on your Rebel List. They should be bigger, more of a stretch. They should be something slightly out of reach, something you would have to really work to accomplish. They should be things that excite you, make you say HELL YES. There should be some items that scare the shit out of you. There should be items that make you think, "I can't possibly do that" or "I am not strong enough to do that". We want you to shudder in your boots. We want you to quiver with expectation.

There is something special that happens in a woman when she sets a galactic goal. She starts to believe. She starts to see that sphere labeled "my world" expand. It envelopes her current reality, making problems smaller, in contrast. Her power drifts out into the world, making her bigger and her influence stronger. If your goal is to pay off your credit card debt, then imagine a flashlight shining down on top of you from the clouds in the dark. Your world view is small. Important to pay off your debt? You bet. But what about this? I am going to help develop a hydroponic gardening system that can be leveraged into developing countries, which will pay me a good salary while helping women of the world…?

So what are you going to do?

Get out a calendar and mark dates of what you want to accomplish over the course of the next 12 to 16 months. If something is going to cost two thousand dollars, push it out a bit and make a plan to create the money to do it.

Be relentless. This list is you. It's what you want. It's your mark on the world. Give up the mental vodka of television and non-stop social media and create something positive. Learn something. Be something. Mark the items with the year you completed them,

As with all the Kiss List items, our goal is to turn-on more women. We want to let them know that all things are possible. We want to pull them into the light. Share your accomplishments on social to prove that creating your legacy is within your grasp.

One fun thing to do is to post all the things you know or have access to, so that other women can draw on you as a resource. Do you live in Bali and know how to play the guitar? Post that in our groups and women who want to travel to Bali or learn guitar can contact you. We lift women up, by doing what we already do.

As with the other items on your Kiss List, when you accomplish them, you get a pin. For Vixen Scarlet, we want you to accomplish three epic goals. Once you do that, we will send you a pin and you can call yourself a proud Vixen.

Examples of Vixen List:

- Lean an instrument then volunteer to play or teach less fortunate people.

- Walk the Camino de Santiago in Spain.

- Build a monument to your grandmother/ mother/sister.

- Create a robot that does something amazing.

- Write a book about your life, your love lessons, your dreams.

- Attend Carnival in Brazil.

- Learn competitive ice-skating.

- Ride the Orient Express.

- Live in a foreign country and publish a photo book about the experience.

- Learn a new dance every day for a year.

- Learn to ski (or snowboard) in Chile.

- Take your mother on an around-the-world trip.

Chapter Ten: Rhinestone Buddy

Do you remember going to the museum when you were in third-grade? You got off the bus in front of the giant building and looked up at the massive columns. Hordes of children ran everywhere, excited to be away from school, if only for a day. You looked around for a familiar face, a friend. Standing above everyone was your teacher, a lovely woman who rocked a crimson set of lips. She wore a yellow dress with flowers on it. She took control of the chaos.

"Everyone, listen to me please!" She clapped her hands once. "Listen." She smiled and everyone exhaled. "I want you to find your museum buddy. Pair up now and if you can't find a partner, come see me."

You always hated this moment, alone in a crowd of kids zooming around like atoms attracted to each other with zero doubt about where to go. From behind the throng of boys punching each other, a smile opens up and a girl you hardly know reaches for your hand.

She says, "Wanna be my museum buddy?"

You relax, grabbing her hand, "Yes please."

You and this girl walk through the museum, hand in hand, platonically watching out for each other, pulling each other through the madness of teasing boys, and dioramas featuring ancient men holding spears while sitting next to a fake fire. You make sure she doesn't get lost. You drink from the fountain together, a team, a tiny pod of hope in a world of possibility too big to grasp. When you return from the museum, back to the reality of spelling tests and chalk dust, you have a bond with this girl. You smile like you both know a silly secret.

Somewhere along the way, we forgot how to do this. We have forgotten what it means to have a museum buddy or swim buddy. We decided that women were not to be trusted. We decided that women were often evil and judgmental Jennifers.

Women treat each other much worse than men. We get together in groups and bitch about other women. "Can you believe what Jenny is doing? OMG." When we don't self-invest, we have nothing to talk about, so we bitch about other women. We fabricate drama to keep ourselves from getting bored. We make up stuff about women to make ourselves feel like we aren't that bad...

In Kick Ass Red Lipstick, this is not allowed.

What is allowed is finding a buddy. We call them Rhinestone Gals. What is a Rhinestone Gal? Essentially they are a museum buddy, for life.

They grab your hand and help you embrace yourself through Kick Ass Red Lipstick. They are leaders, pulling us out of the mud, dusting us off, and giving us purpose and engagement. How does it work?

Here are the steps:

1. Once you are a member of Kick Ass Red Lipstick, find a woman you think will benefit from some lipstick therapy, some booty-kicking, woman-power.

2. Invite her to participate.

3. Tell her if she likes what she sees, you will be her mentor, holding her hand as her Rhinestone Gal.

4. Introduce her to the group of women in your area's Kick Ass Red Lipstick chapter.

5. Help her go through the Kiss List transformation.

6. You earn a Rhinestone for every woman you mentor.

When women are challenged with opportunities that are outside the box, they often find it difficult to proceed without support. In my studio, I know women never walk through the doors by themselves. They always come with a "buddy" to help soften the intensity of doing something out of the norm. This is similar for Kick Ass Red Lipstick. Being a Rhinestone Gal is an important part of the Kick Ass legacy. Do you remember going to your first meeting and not knowing anyone? Maybe you had questions or comments but you felt too intimidated to voice your opinion? We don't want this for the beauties of Kick Ass. As women who empower and support other women, we need to give our girlfriends permission to come on this journey with us. Not only will she benefit from this experience, but so will you.

Chapter Eleven: Clever Leverage

So let's assume we have a woman who is exceptional at being a Rhinestone Gal. She loves helping women transform themselves with the power of Kick Ass Red Lipstick. Next thing she knows, her sister, mother, daughter, and her gal-pals from college are wearing red lipstick. Maybe she is mid-way through her Kiss List Journey.

What should she do next?

She could start her own local Kick Ass Red Lipstick Chapter.

Think about it. You have gone to a job for YEARS. You started a family. You started dinner. What else have you started? (I was in this exact same boat a few years ago…)

How about starting something that is a true reflection of you? What can you start today that would shock you? What can you start in your area that allows other women to be amazed by their own actions?

We know the answer: A local Kick Ass Red Lipstick Chapter.

There are instructions on our website, but there are a couple of things to note. To begin with, you are going to use Quintessence to name your own chapter. Name your group after your own sense of style. If you are a super-hero-gal, search for a super hero team name generator online. League of Rebellious Vixens? Quintessential Gathering of Super Gals? If you like a certain color of lipstick, name it as inspired by that color (mind trademarks, ladies). Rapscallion Reds? Name it something awesome, or silly, or dramatic, or classic. The choice is yours.

What do you do at meetings? Whatever you want. An easy place to farm ideas is the Kiss List. You can start a Kiss List for your group. Just apply the same process as the individual transformation listed above. So what Blushing Pink activities do you want to do as a group? What Rebel Rouge journey do you want to take on? Do you want to take a group road trip? Do you want to all go skydiving, skinny-dipping, or singing show tunes door-to-door in June? What legacy items can you create as a group? What Vixen list items can you create as a group that could change the world?

Let's say you have a new member who is just starting with Kick Ass, perhaps your group can go with her to get her nails done. Can you imagine thirty women in Kick Ass Red Lipstick showing up at a nail salon, supporting their new friend?

Which brings us to the next step in our Rhinestone Journey. We all have skills. Every one of us. Some of us are dancers and some of us are sculptors.

Some of us are Master Gardeners. Some of us are architects, advertising mavens, hot air balloon specialists, or glass blowers.

Can you show another woman how to do what you do? If you are a glass blower and you have a studio, you could host a group of Lipstick gals at your shop and teach them the basics of glass blowing, correct? HELL YES you could. So stick with me (pun intended).

Back a few pages ago, we talked about your Kiss List. You were asked to come up with a wide range of items you needed to accomplish. So you have all these things you want to do before you die and we have a whole group of women who do a lot of these things professionally or as hobbies.

So we put the women who are working on their Kiss Lists, together with the women of the Kick Ass Red Lipstick and we have magic.

Let's say you have on your Kiss List that you want to travel to New Zealand. Well, you can find a member of Kick Ass Red Lipstick that is a Kiwi who can help you with the best places to visit.

Let's say you want to learn to paint flowers like Georgia O'Keefe. You look for someone in our organization that is an accomplished painter and ask for help. You both win, as you learn how to paint and she learns more about herself by teacher you her passion.

You want to learn how to race cars? You want to fly a plane? You want to dance burlesque? We have people for that. When you reach out in vulnerability, you open yourself up to new expanses of self-investment.

You know how to build a blog or adopt a child or change careers at forty? You pull yourself up by helping and teaching another woman. You become part of their story and they become part of yours.

What do we call women who start their own chapters or help other women accomplish their Kiss Lists? Rhinestone Gals. For every woman you help, either by bringing them into your chapter or helping them with their Kiss List, you earn a Rhinestone.

Chapter Twelve: Legastory

In the previous sections, we have focused on creating value for you by self-investing, exploring your legacy and having some fucking fun...

In this section, we want to bring it back around to the people who love you, who respect you, who you look after, who dream with you. The stories of your interaction with these people are one of the legacies of your life. They are treasure boxes filled with dreams, dramas, and love. Your stories make up Kick Ass Red Lipstick.

We invite you to create your story. We want you to inspire yourself and the ones who love you by writing down your experiences, or making art, or writing a letter. We want to pull you into a space where you can create your story and leave it for the next generation, so your family can see who you were, what you were about, three hundred years from now. Our stories make up who we are. They are our legacies in words and pictures.

How do you do that? Take your journal and start writing. Write your mother or daughter a letter. Pull out your phone and make a video about your life. Tell the story about what you have endured as a woman...either to share wisdom or to tell someone you appreciate them.

I wrote a note a day for my mother while she was in chemotherapy. Every day she arrived, she opened a new note. She found out what I admired about her, important lessons I learned from her, and times when I was grateful for her. I told her I loved her, over and over, not just by using the words, but by telling the story of us. It is something I will always remember, a bond that made us stronger and closer. Gifts are more than just things…the gift of ourselves, our thoughts, and our love can be the greatest gifts of all.

You can do this too.

Here are the steps:

1. Find some place to archive your story. Some women like to email their story to themselves or keep it in a cloud-based service, so they know they will never lose it. Some women prefer a journal. Some like video. It doesn't matter what the method or recording your story is. Just find a method you are comfortable with.

2. Pick a time to write. I like mornings.

3. Sit down and write. Write about the time you fell off the horse at camp. Write about having to help your mother out with rent money by working a job after school. Write about

anything you want. Write about what happened to you yesterday.

4. Encourage your parents to write down their story, so you can learn from them and your children's children can learn from them.

5. Share your story with someone. Let your family know where the stories are kept.

Maybe writing isn't for you or you can't take the time to write or make videos. Can you think of another way you can create and share your story with your loved ones?

Your actions.

We have all heard the saying, "actions speak louder than words". This rang in my head over and over when I was married. The words coming out of his mouth never matched his actions. I would always think, "He tells me he loves me, yet doesn't show me". We have all been in relationships like this. We end up burned-out because we are the constant givers and the only thing we ever had to base our actions on, was that they said they "loved" us.

Actions are important in Kick Ass Red Lipstick. You act upon your dreams and desires in order to move up to the ultimate Vixen status. We want you to be able to set a good example for women of what a true Kick Ass woman is about. Want to leave your story behind with your actions? You can.

I often tell my students a life lesson my mother taught me at a young age. If you are having a bad day and nothing is helping… do something for someone else. There is nothing more rewarding, uplifting, soul-filling than to make someone else's day. You leave a legacy by being a warrior who can overcome bad days and do something special for someone else. Mind you, this does not include everyday events that we do to help our family and friends. This is something different…unique…a pattern break both for you and the special someone.

Although doing things for strangers can be rewarding, like paying for the person's drink behind you in the coffee shop, adopting a family during the holidays, or donating to a local charity – I am talking about the special Kick Ass women in your life. As women, we are naturally givers. Yet some women have proven they don't want kindness. I am not talking about them. I am talking about those who do deserve it. We all have different battles as women and we all deserve to be appreciated even when it isn't expected. Do you want to leave a legacy as someone who was positive, empowered, and loving of the women in your life so that they can tell stories about you for generations? What type of example would you like to leave for your daughter? Think about it, then take action!

Chapter Thirteen: Lasting Friendships

As previously stated, women are in constant competition with each other. Why? There is a saying that circulates social media:

"I wish women would treat each other in the real world the way they treat each other in the women's restroom."

A few years ago, I went on a first date with a man I had met on an online dating site. We decided to go to dinner and to take a walk in the park. While at dinner, we talked about our online profiles and whether or not we were what we expected (this is a common conversation in the online dating world).

Him: "Am I what you expected?"

Me: "Yes, am I?"

Him: "Not really. You are much bigger than I anticipated."

My heart sank. I was honest with my online profile, even stating "curvy" as my body type. At that time, I was trying to sort out my life, including my weight. I could not believe he had said such awful words to me. I felt alone and wanted to leave. I didn't eat my dinner and asked to be excused to go to the bathroom. Once I was inside, I started crying.

Within seconds I had two women, one on each side, asking me what happened. I told them the story.

"You are gorgeous! Don't listen to him"

"I can't believe he said that! He doesn't deserve you"

"If I were you, I would walk out right now"

You get the picture. It's crazy – we bond in the powder room. Why is that? Why are we so kind, encouraging, and loving to each other in the bathroom, yet once we step out of that sacred space we rip each other to shreds? It's like it is a portal that takes us to another reality. In the bathroom, women unite and are a force to be reckoned with. Outside the restroom, it's every women for herself.

I tell my students over and over again. Each woman is on her own journey. Before you act like a mean girl to the gal across the room, ask yourself what you would say to her in the powder room? You would tell her how much you loved everything about her. I know you would. My mission is to change this way of thinking, to build earth shattering bonds with our sisters, in and out

80

of the powder room. We are here to build you up and stop the tide of mean girls.

There is an old adage that says that people who survive a plane crash together create a bond that is uncommon. They have a connection that people who haven't been through that drama do not have. They are sisters and brothers in a special way.

I would like to posit that we, as women, share a similar bond. Not all of us have survived a plane crash, but we have all survived being women, which is beyond a blessing, but often a difficult row to hoe. I wouldn't change who I am or my experiences for any amount of money. I love being a woman. But admit it, between the two sexes, we are the ones who have survived the plane crash. We have been abused, ridiculed, second class citizens for millennia. We have been used, destroyed, blamed, and thrown away since the dawn of time. We have survived the proverbial plane crash.

It takes bravery to post a selfie in Kick Ass Red Lipstick. It takes bravery to look at your life via the Kiss List. It takes bravery to start your own Kick Ass Red Lipstick chapter and earn your pins. So when we see women come into our group, we know what it feels like. We remember posting our first selfie. We remember putting on red lipstick for the first time. So it is our mission to reach out and embrace women, to create lasting and real relationships with people who are just like us. To reach out to women who might be suffering or looking to change their lives.

Don't get me wrong, I am not arguing for a victim mentality. I am not saying, "Gee whiz, ain't it hard to be a woman". All I am saying is, we have survived and we can join together under the banner of Kick Ass Red Lipstick. We can develop real friendships. We can live up to our mandate to protect ourselves and those we love. We have the opportunity to create something positive and move away from our life's trauma. We can create a space for us to live in, based on what we want and who want to be.

We can be women. We can be friends. We can be free.

Chapter Fourteen: Pillars of Awesome

Did your mother yell at you when you acted like an idiot in front of your little sister? Did your grandmother grab your earlobe and twist, yell-whispering in your ear about, "are we setting a good example"? Well, here is your opportunity…

Kick Ass Red Lipstick and the Lipstick Society is a group of women opting to create something that sets the example for generations of young (and old) women. Can you be part of something that changes history? It will be challenging, but it will also be a kick in the pants.

Imagine telling your thirteen year old daughter that you are part of a group of women designed to empower and change lives and that it is based entirely on the foundation of red lipstick? How would that make you feel? Maybe a little like a super hero, a secret agent, or a guardian? You could bring your daughter into the organization and educate her on the power of lipstick, on the power of sensuality for her own sake, not for the sake of society, a man, or for what she thinks she has to do. Kick Ass Red Lipstick is not only a society for women. Kick Ass Red Lipstick is looking to change the way women think. ALL women. We want to set positive examples so women can see the freedom and life-changing experiences that Kick Ass Red Lipstick can bring them.

How would it make you feel if after you started your Kiss List and you accomplished some items, a young woman in your office came up to you and told you how much you inspired her? What if she said, because of you, that she was taking a class that she had always wanted to take, wearing that skirt she had always wanted to wear, or was finally standing up for herself to her boyfriend?

At my last corporate job, I did not let my position or duties define who I was. I would dress how I wanted to dress every morning – high heel shoes, skirts, blouses and of course, my Kick Ass Red Lipstick. I would hear versions of this all the time –

"Why are you so dressed up?"

"I could never wear heels like that."

"You style is so… trendy."

"Where do you get your clothes from?"

"We wonder every day… what will Cat wear tomorrow?"

I admit, it did bother me at times. I felt like I was being picked on because I was different. I did not wear khaki pants, boring suits, or pajama bottoms and a sweatshirt – I had my own style. I expressed who I was through my clothing and no matter what was said, it wasn't going to change. I would always say to myself, "They hired me knowing I was like this. I am not changing." Then something amazing happened:

The women in the office started dressing up.

I was rubbing off on them. Since I dressed the way I wanted, they felt they could do the same. Heels were being worn, chunky necklaces, spots and stripes, and even skirts.

My boss said, "See what you've done to us?"

I knew exactly what I did. I gave them permission (we will cover more about the power of permission in a few chapters).

How would you feel if you started self-investing again and people started to notice, people could see the anger and emotional swelling drop from your face to be replaced by joy, a rebellious finger against all the shit we think we need to be? It's one of the reasons Kick Ass Red Lipstick is so powerful: when a woman starts to self-invest, transformation begins. Be prepared – you will be stopped and asked things like:

"Did you change your hair?"

"Did you lose weight?"

"Are those new clothes?"

The only thing that changed is your perception of yourself. You are loving you, and others recognize this. You are a walking role model for women who are afraid to do something for themselves. Not only are you transforming yourself, but you are helping those women around you jumpstart their own transformation. You are giving them permission to be themselves…finally.

How would it feel to put lipstick on your little girl, who was suffering from cancer, bald yet smiling as the lipstick that mommy wears is the only thing that makes her smile.

Sometimes the person you inspire might surprise you.

Chapter Fifteen: Thistle

We all know boys. Some of us have met some men. On some levels, men are brilliant and inspired creatures. Some of them are disgusting lumps of festering damage, who only help us when they get out of our way. However, men, as a group, have some lovely ideas. One of them is honor.

What is honor? Men think it's dying for their country or opening a door for lady. They talk a lot about being honorable in all sorts of war-bound, inflated tones. We love men, don't get us wrong. But for us, we think about the word a little differently.

This is a group of women. We can either self-regulate or rip ourselves apart. We understand that with a large group of women, this could easily devolve into a Festival of Jennifers, a wide-eyed, bleach-blonde bullshit war.

What we want instead, is to bring women into a space where they love (honor) themselves and then don't feel the need to attack other women. And when they are around other like-minded women, they honor (love) them in a way that creates space for both women to thrive.

So we think it's important, vital almost, that women are able to self-manage. All of these things, the Kiss List, et al, are based on your honor. We will not, cannot come out to verify if you are who you say you are. If you are a lie, only you will pay the price.

This leads us into the next housekeeping area: mean girls.

We are a women's empowerment organization. We are a lipstick-rocking, hip-chick, dream hammer. What we see (on occasion) is women who begin the Kiss List a little damaged, shy, psychologically under the weather, but emerge as raging assholes, confusing bitchiness for empowerment. As one of our husbands put it, "Just because women come out of their shell, doesn't mean they are pretty on the inside."

When you are wearing Kick Ass Red Lipstick, the challenge is to be humble, put together, and aware. It's easy to walk through the world as Jennifer, hair-flipping and gossiping your way from one bitch session to another. What takes guts is opening up and embracing yourself and subsequently embracing other women.

We do not tolerate negative talk about women, any woman, including yourself. If you are here to find a sewing group of snarky know-it-alls, move along please. Nothing to see here.

We are not here to be your mother. If you can't operate with honor, that's on you. If you are a liar, a mean girl, a negative Jennifer, that's on you. We have tools to help pull you out of that slump, but we are not here to mother you. Get your act together, for you, so you can come and have some fun with us.

Chapter Sixteen: My Permission

Can you remember the first time you jumped off the diving board on your own? You stood there, unsure, unable to jump. Your best friend called from the inside of the pool. Tears welled up in your eyes, a drifting pull yanked at your insides, urging you to run away, it wasn't worth it. You were terrified.

On the other hand, you knew that making it off the diving board put you in a special club, a group of elite girls, the brave ones who could run off the end of the diving board like they were launching into space, scream-laughing all the way.

You looked around the room for a friendly face. The life guard whistled at you, indicating you should jump or get off the board. You began to panic. But your eyes landed on your grandmother's smile, sitting on a bench on the side of the pool. She was everything you ever wanted to be: classy, jubilant at the right times, and brutally strong at others. She grinned at you and every muscle relaxed in your body and the tears came harder, but their label changed from fear to power. Grandmother was too far away for you to hear her, so she simply nodded her head in permission, to say, "You can do it".

You took two steps back, and ran off the end of the board. You sat under water for a moment, smiling. Finally you shot up out of the surface, like a new mermaid. You found your grandmother's eyes again and she winked, like making it off the diving board was a sparkly gift that you held in your hands since birth, but you just had to open your fingers to see it.

Which brings us to our next rung in the ladder: Social Norms and Permission.

Social norms or expectations laid on us by society are evident from birth. We see how other women behave and we want to emulate, to fit in, to be one of the cool kids. This is a survival mechanism in group sociology – decide not to be different, and the likelihood of being eaten reduces. But at this point, our hierarchy of needs has all the basics handled. At this point, social norms are more about fitting in, being just like every other white Cadillac SUV driving, sparkle jeans wearing Jennifer than it is about surviving.

Take a moment and think about where you are complying with unwritten social norms. Any of this sound familiar? We rush off to college (which is probably a good thing), graduate and land in a cubicle, sacrificing our lives for the next forty years to a company that doesn't give a singular shit about anything but your output (which they shouldn't: their mission is to generate profits, not friends). We shouldn't blame companies, we should blame ourselves.

How about the uniforms we wear? Next time you are at the grocery store, look at the outfits women wear. Can you tell who they are, based on what they are wearing? Can you see what stage of life they are in? Do you wear sparkle jeans and a sweatshirt from your kid's athletic program? Ball cap and t-shirt from the local college you didn't attend? Pajama pants to the grocery store? Yoga pants when you don't actually work out, at all…? What are you saying to the world with your uniform? I know the answer most women give is that they dress this way to feel comfortable. It's only the store, no reason to bother…

The problem starts when this becomes the norm and it is a special occasion thing for you to dress up, to look nice, to wear a Kick Ass Red Lipstick. Not because of what other people will think, but what you think. Looking good, having your situation tight, is part of self-investment.

I had someone I care about deeply come up to me after I gave birth to my first child and say, "You're a mom now. You need to cut your hair short."

"What? Why?"

She said, "Well, that's just what moms do. And it will be easier to wash and the baby will have a harder time grabbing it."

Short hair is not a good look for me. I love my children, but cutting my hair just to fit in with the mom club is crazy. There is NOTHING that says that when you have a baby you have to cut your hair.

What other uniforms do we wear? Do you see a husband and wife and you can't tell which is which because they are wearing almost the same clothes? Jeans, t-shirt, running shoes, and maybe a ball cap? Now, some of you are going to pipe up for women's right to be comfortable, or equality in dress. If you are arguing that, then you haven't understood the point of this book. Red lipstick can break those patterns and allow us to feel pretty, to be girly again. It's OK to be girly. Equality is great, as it relates to pay, rights, etc. But men, in general, dress like they are going to work at the dump. It's not a good look to copy...

And if you were going to argue for always dressing comfortable, I am certain that men do not want to sleep with a masculine version of their wife. They chased you around, as a woman, not a frumpy version of themselves.

How about your lingerie? Does your man buy you lingerie or expect you to dress a certain way in order to get in the mood? This is a uniform. I understand that people need to spice up their relationships after many years, but take a look at your lingerie and think about what it says about you, your relationship. I wear night-gowns, I get it. But I do not need to wear something to get my man in the mood. If you are going to shop at Victoria's Secret, buy what you want to wear, what makes you feel pretty and your partner will see that you are happy and sexy.

You can grow your hair out. I give you permission. You can buy the sensual lingerie you want to wear and wear it for you, not them. I give you permission. You can go through your closet and donate all the frumpy crap that makes you feel like a walking pill bug. I give you permission. You can buy yourself some clothes that fit. I give you permission. You can buy yourself some Kick Ass Red Lipstick. You can get your physical health in order, for you. I give you permission.

I hear some of you saying, "Jason won't let me." Oh, I see, your husband or your boyfriend is your keeper... He won't let you? If this is the case, I would argue that you have a bigger problem. This is no longer the 1950s. If you live in a country where this is your current reality, be brave, be bold, rock some Kick Ass Red Lipstick and tell your man, who really wants to be your daddy, to go fuck himself.

We are not cattle. We cannot be owned. There are laws which we have to abide by, but short of that, nobody has any right to expect anything from you, unless you allow it. Yes, we have responsibilities, and we deal with those in different ways. However, to say that your man won't allow you to wear lipstick, or won't allow you to wear dresses or gets upset when you look pretty, is completely not allowed.

If you find yourself in a situation where someone is controlling, manipulative, and jealous, perhaps you need to take a closer look at your life. Why are you with someone like that? Have you changed since you got involved with them? Is this situation good for you? If someone behaves like this, as it relates to how you look and dress, there will be other issues inside the relationship.

I got out. So can you.

Women are taught that they need men to live. Many women have been in relationships with men, with little or no breaks, since they were teenagers. This is crazy behavior. If you have not lived alone, I challenge you to consider this a pivotal step in your growth. It's hard to know yourself if you have never spent any time alone. This takes us back to our Kiss List. What do you do for fun?

If you don't know who you are, how can you expect someone else to know who you are? We do this nasty thing, as women, where we don't know ourselves, then we get angry at our spouses for not understanding us...

One reason our relationships suck is that our relationship with ourselves is terrible. We can't bear to look in the mirror, can't bear to be alone, so we look for the nearest lifeboat, which is often another crap relationship. If we were to self-invest to the point where we love ourselves and know ourselves, we would attract the right relationship, one that doesn't come in a lifeboat.

After my divorce, I was single for six years before I found my man. I worked on myself. I changed the way I carried myself. I started a business. I lost weight. I raised my kids. I grew to know me again, without the light of someone else shinning down on me. I took myself on dates. I worked through my Kiss List (before it was called Kiss List).

People would ask me what was wrong with me? Why are you still single? I was single by choice. I would much rather be in a relationship with myself than be in the wrong relationship. I was working on me. I was trying different options, getting used to saying no. I had already been in one difficult marriage. I was not eager to repeat that mistake.

We get lost in our roles. We become these terms: mother, girlfriend, cook, lover, cleaner, caregiver, driver, nurse, and wife. Once you can take a step back and evaluate which roles are meaningful to you, you can create yourself in your own image. After a divorce or breakup, we need time to connect with who we are, before we take on new roles.

You do not have settle. You do not have to accept someone treating you poorly. If your husband or boyfriend/girlfriend is a dick, leave them. I give you permission to stand up for yourself and do some housekeeping. We, as the Lipstick Society, will stand behind you and support you, holding a Kick Ass Red Lipstick ready when you decide that nobody can tell you not to wear lipstick.

Conclusion

In the beginning, we start out as young girls, full of sparkles and possibilities. Somewhere along the line, we fall into a trap or two. If we are lucky, someone hands us a book like this that can pull us out of the trap. If we are lucky there are women who will come to our aid, pointing us in the direction of change.

Kick Ass Red Lipstick is a way for us to become who we are truly meant to be. Kick Ass Red Lipstick is the framework for you to leave your legacy. Kick Ass Red Lipstick is a way to make lasting friends, to start up something that you can be proud of. We are a group of like-minded power gals. We sincerely hope you join us in our struggle to expand our lives, change the world, and have a Kick Ass time.

Hugs, Cat

Glossary

- Blushing Pink: The first part of the Kiss List that encourages women to find small, easily accomplishable tasks they can do to self-invest, to do something for them. Like getting a new Kick Ass Red Lipstick or a manicure.

- Blushettes: After completing ten items on our Blushing Pink List, we become recognized by the Lipstick Society as a Blushette and receive a lapel pin to commemorate our accomplishment.

- Jason: A man who typically wears the same thing as every other male, loves all sports but doesn't play any, says "bro" often, has a large truck, lots of guns, and a disgusting attitude. Can be seen associating with Jennifers.

- Jennifer: A woman who is mimicking all the pretty Barbie girls around her. Thin, bleach blonde, big fake boobs, stupid SUV, sparkle jeans, etc. Can be seen associating with Jason.

- Kick Ass Red Lipstick Chapter: Women are starting their own Kick Ass Red Lipstick groups in their local areas around the country.

- Kiss List: A list that is broken up into three parts (small items, fun items, and legacy items) that our women work through in order to change their lives.

- Quintessence: Process to name yourself, to create your new avatar. Can also be used to name a chapter.

- Rebel Rouge: Second part of the Kiss List, encouraging women to find what is fun in their lives and to go do it.

- Rebels: After completing five items off their Rebel Rouge List, our gals can be recognized as Rebels and receive a pin from Kick Ass Red Lipstick.

- Rhinestone Gals: Women who act as mentors for other women in Kick Ass Red Lipstick.

- Vixen Scarlet: Third part of the Kiss List, encouraging women to establish their epic or legacy ideas and to make a plan to make their dreams come true.

- Vixens : After completing three items off their Vixen Scarlet List, our gals can be recognized as Vixens and receive a pin from Kick Ass Red Lipstick.

Made in the USA
San Bernardino, CA
02 February 2016